A Teacher's Calendar Companion

OCTOBER

Creative Ideas to Enrich Monthly Plans!

WRITTEN BY
Wendy Roh Jenks

Cover Illustration by
Dan Sharp

Inside Illustrations by
Becky Radtke

Published by Instructional Fair • TS Denison
an imprint of
McGraw-Hill Children's Publishing

About the Author

Wendy Roh Jenks has a bachelor's degree in language arts and elementary education and a master's degree in reading from Grand Valley State University. Currently in her ninth year of teaching, Wendy teaches third grade in Rockford, Michigan. She has done extensive editing for Instructional Fair • TS Denison. Wendy wrote all ten books in the *A Teacher's Calendar Companion* series.

Credits
Author: Wendy Roh Jenks
Inside Illustrator: Becky Radtke
Cover Artist: Dan Sharp
Cover Design: Annette Hollister-Papp
Project Director/Editor: Sara Bierling
Editors: Mary Hassinger, Alyson Kieda
Graphic Layout: Tracy L. Wesorick

McGraw-Hill
Children's Publishing
A Division of The McGraw-Hill Companies

Send all inquiries to:
McGraw-Hill Children's Publishing
3195 Wilson Drive NW
Grand Rapids, Michigan 49544

Printed in the United States of America

A Teacher's Calendar Companion: October
ISBN: 0-7424-0185-5

1 2 3 4 5 6 7 8 9 05 04 03 02 01

TABLE OF CONTENTS

MORNING ROUTINE

Having something prepared for students to do when they first come in the room frees you to do morning housekeeping tasks, such as reading parent notes, collecting lunch money, and taking attendance. Here are some spooky activities to get your October days started right.

ACTIVITY-A-DAY

Use these motivating but simple activities to get your students on track first thing in the morning. Page 5 contains twenty-five activities suitable for grades K–1 students. Page 6 contains twenty-five activities suitable for students in grades 2–3. Duplicate the appropriate page for your class and use one of the following ideas to manage the selection of activities.

Activity Calendar

Duplicate the appropriate activity sheet once. Cut out each rectangle. Cut twenty-five rectangles out of construction paper. Fold each rectangle in half. Glue one activity inside each folded rectangle. Hang the activities on a calendar so there is one activity for each school day this month.

Individual Calendars

Duplicate the appropriate activity sheet once for each student. Students cut apart the activities and glue them on their own calendars in any order they choose. Each day, students consult their own calendars for their activity choices.

Envelope of Activities

Duplicate the appropriate activity sheet once for each student. Students cut apart the activities and place them in an envelope. Each day, students choose one activity from their envelopes. Have students glue their activity squares to the top of the papers on which they complete the activities.

Activity Journals

Make a journal for each student by stapling lined paper between two construction-paper covers. Students date the page before completing each activity.

Enlarge and Post the Activity

Use a copy machine to enlarge each activity so it can be posted on a bulletin board. Make a special spot on the bulletin board where the students look each morning for the designated activity of the day.

MORNING MOTIVATORS

Question of the Day

Write a question on the chalkboard each morning for students to answer in their journals. Relate questions to a current social studies, science, or math topic. Questions could also be basic trivia.

Riddle of the Day

Students read and respond to a riddle or joke that has been written on the chalkboard or overhead projector.

Language Activity

Write a sentence on the chalkboard with several grammar or spelling mistakes. Students copy the sentence and make the appropriate corrections.

Finish the Picture

Draw part of a picture or shape on the chalkboard. Have the students copy the drawing and complete the picture.

ACTIVITY BOARD ACTIVITIES

GRADES K-1

Cut three words from a magazine that start with the letter *O*. 	Draw a picture of trick-or-treaters. 	Draw and color the Earth. 	Count the number of letters in the name *Columbus*. 	Draw a pumpkin for each year of your age. 
Draw and decorate a Halloween mask. 	Make a Halloween bookmark. 	Draw a house. 	Count the number of letters in the word *Halloween*. 	Draw one of Columbus's ships. 
Draw your Halloween costume. 	Draw a picture of a fire-fighter. 	Tell a friend about some-thing that she can do to prevent fires. 	Create a Halloween card. 	Finish this sentence: "Halloween is..." 
Draw a picture of a place you would like to discover. 	Write a spooky story. 	Cut three words from the newspaper that start with the letter *B*. 	Draw a big spider with eight legs. 	Design your own jack-o'-lantern. 
Practice "stop, drop, and roll." 	Find three words that rhyme with the word *boo*. 	Create or copy a recipe that uses apples. 	Draw a bat. 	Draw and color a picture of a candy factory. 

ACTIVITY BOARD ACTIVITIES

GRADES 2–3

Write five words using the letters in the word *October*.	List safety rules for trick-or-treating.	Draw and color the Earth.	List ten things Columbus might have seen when he arrived in America.	Draw a pumpkin patch with a pumpkin for each year of your age.
Draw a tree. Write five math problems with sums of 10 on the leaves.	Write five questions that begin with the word *Who*.	Design a house.	Count the vowels and consonants in the word *Halloween*. Add the two numbers.	Draw Christopher Columbus's three ships.
Use art paper to design a fall bookmark.	Draw a picture of your Halloween costume.	Design a fire-safety poster.	List five ways to help prevent fires.	Use art paper to design a Halloween card.
Finish this story: "As the kids walked slowly to the old house..."	Finish this sentence: "Fall is..."	Write a story about a land you would like to discover.	Design your own jack-o'-lantern.	Write eight words that rhyme with the word *bat*. Use them in a "batty" poem.
Write a letter to a candy maker.	Draw a big spider with eight legs. Write a spooky word on each leg.	Draw a map showing where you will go trick-or-treating.	Create a recipe that uses apples.	Write a story about a magic broom.

OCTOBER CALENDARS

Classroom Calendar

Reinforce calendar concepts and support your math curriculum by having a classroom calendar. Set aside time each day to discuss skills appropriate to your classroom needs. Here are some activities to do during calendar time.

- Identify today, yesterday, and tomorrow.
- Identify the date.
- Keep track of how many school days have passed with a number line and tallies. Teach place value by looking for number patterns.
- Look at patterns created on the calendar by using a combination of shapes and colors for the dates.
- Identify birthdays, holidays, or other special events. Count days remaining until the events. Have students predict what pattern shape will fall on a certain day.
- Record the day's weather.
- Talk about different ways to represent the number of the date. For example, on October 12, students may list 6 + 6, one dozen, or 4 x 3.
- Write on date shapes to keep track of important events for the month. Create a journal of the month's activities by gluing the shapes into an October book.

Individual Student Calendar

Duplicate page 8 for each student. Use this calendar in a variety of ways. Choose one or two of the following activities to complement class studies.

- On the first day of the month, write in the dates for the whole month. Add special assignments and events.
- Each day, write the date. Fill in weekend dates on Mondays.
- Each morning, have students name the day and date, yesterday's day and date, and tomorrow's day and date.
- Maintain a design pattern across the calendar days. For example, have students draw a fall leaf on day one, a pumpkin on day two, and a candy corn on day three. Students should repeat the pattern throughout the month and look for diagonal and vertical patterns that develop.
- On each calendar day, students write different ways to represent that number. For example, on October 24, students could write 23 + 1, 12 x 2, 50 – 26, or two dozen.
- Use the calendar as a class incentive chart. Place stickers on student calendars for good behavior or great work.
- Use the calendar as a class incentive chart. At the end of the month, students may be awarded candy corns if they have earned a given number of stickers. Stickers may be earned for good behavior and good work.

OCTOBER

SUNDAY	MONDAY	TUESDAY	WEDNESDAY	THURSDAY	FRIDAY	SATURDAY

COMMUNICATION/PARENT CONNECTIONS

Newsletters

Send home a weekly newsletter to regularly communicate with parents what is happening in the classroom. See pages 11 and 12 for reproducible outlines of weekly newsletters. The following are different approaches to communication with parents.

1. On Monday, send home a newsletter that indicates the major themes, skills, books, and events of the upcoming week. Use the outline on page 11. At home, students complete the sentences at the bottom of the page about their week at school. This is a great way for students to reflect on the important events and lessons of the week. Have students return the sentences at the beginning of the following week.
2. On Friday, send home the newsletter on page 11 with the lessons, books, and events of the past week. Have students help you write the newsletter. Duplicate the completed newsletter for each student. Have them finish the sentences on the bottom of the page before they take it home.
3. Send home a newsletter that is based on the skills, themes, and events of each curriculum area you will be studying in the upcoming or past week. Have the students help you write the newsletter, and/or ask students to add illustrations. Use the reproducible outline on page 12.

Daily Log

When parents ask, "What did you do today?," they often hear "I don't know." Help students form their answers in advance by writing a daily log. Students fill out a daily log at the end of each day with a description of the most important events of the day (see page 13 for a daily log). Younger students may copy a sentence from the chalkboard or draw a picture. As an alternative, end your day with a brainstorming session about what the class learned that day. Write student responses in the outline on page 13. Reproduce the Daily Log to send home on Friday.

Quality-Time Activities

Give parents ideas of quality activities they can do at home with their children. At the beginning of the month, send home the October Quality-Time Activities sheet on page 14.

Reading Log

To encourage at-home reading, send home a reading log. Keep track of the books students have read during the month (see page 15). Older students may read and record their own books while younger students may record books others have read to them. When students return the logs at the end of the month, have them share their favorite books with the rest of the class. Offer a small incentive, such as a bookmark, for each returned reading log. A pizza lunch may be awarded at the end of a semester or the school year for those who returned all their logs for a given period of time.

MORE CONNECTIONS

Sharing Bag

A sharing bag can be a cloth bag, backpack, or even a brown paper bag that goes home with each student in the class—one at a time. Each time it goes home, the student works with his or her family to add to the bag according to the directions. The next day, the student shares his or her work with the rest of the class and passes the bag on to the next student. To add interest, put other related items in the bag, such as a book, a plush toy, or a treat. One of the wonderful results of the sharing bag is that students and their families look forward to seeing what is in the bag, reading other students' work, and adding to the bag. Modify the directions below to reflect the needs and interests of your students. Younger students may need to dictate the story to parents to be written in the notebook. As part of the morning routine, have the student share what he or she added to the sharing bag the previous evening.

For October's sharing bag activity, place a small pumpkin or a tag board pumpkin in the bag. Include a notebook with the following directions glued to the inside front cover.

Dear Parents,

Help your child decorate the enclosed pumpkin to look like a person. You may use any materials you have at home—markers, yarn, buttons, glitter, etc. On the next available clean page in the notebook, help your child write a story about the character you have created. Feel free to enjoy reading the other journal entries made so far. Return the notebook and the pumpkin in the sharing bag on the next school day. Your child will be sharing his or her creation with the rest of the class. Thank you for your help!

Sincerely,

Awards and Incentives

Use awards and incentive charts to give your students positive feedback and to build self-esteem (see pages 16 and 17 for examples). The incentive chart may be used individually or as a class to keep track of progress toward a specific goal. Place stickers in the squares as progress is made. Reward students with extra recess time, a no-homework pass, free time, or lunch with the teacher.

The stationery on pages 18 and 19 can be used for notes to parents, students, or other staff members. Use the stationery in the printer to create classroom posters and signs.

Name ____________________

THIS WEEK'S NEWS FROM ROOM

Monday
Tuesday
Wednesday
Thursday
Friday

For Your Information ____________________

____

Looking Back at My Week

The most important thing I learned this week was ____________________

____________________.

The thing I need to continue to work on the most is ____________________

____________________.

I did something nice for someone when I ____________________

____________________.

One word to describe my week is ____________________.

Name ______________________

THIS WEEK'S NEWS FROM ROOM

Math	**Reading**
Science	**Writing**
Spelling	**Social Studies**

Name ____________________

DAILY LOG

Week of ____________________

Monday
Tuesday
Wednesday
Thursday
Friday

Notes for Next Week

OCTOBER QUALITY-TIME ACTIVITIES

Do one of the following activities with your child each day in October.

1. Find orange and black things at home.
2. Go to the library and check out Halloween books. Read together.
3. Find Halloween candy ads in the newspaper. Compare prices.
4. Help your child create a pumpkin poem.
5. Have your child write words using the letters in the word *Halloween.*
6. Start a story. Have your child finish it.
7. Ask your child to name or write words that rhyme with the word *bat.*
8. Practice the "stop, drop, and roll" technique.
9. Have a fire drill.
10. Develop a fire escape plan. Practice it.
11. Look up five adjectives in the dictionary.
12. Discuss Columbus Day. Ask your child to draw Columbus's three ships.
13. Use candy corn to make math problems for your child to solve.
14. Have your child name three words that begin with each letter in the word *October.*
15. Count aloud 1–50 (by 1s, 2s, 5s, or 10s). Ask your child to say "Boo" when you omit a number.
16. Rake leaves into a pile. Jump in!
17. Have your child draw a fall picture. Cut into puzzle pieces. Help your child put the picture together again.
18. Collect fall leaves and press between wax paper with a warm iron.
19. Have your child draw five pumpkins, each with a different facial expression.
20. Go on a voyage of discovery. Help your child plan a journey to a far-off land.
21. Help your child make Halloween cards using orange and black paper, crayons, and scissors.
22. Carve a jack-o'-lantern with your child's help. Save seeds and count them.
23. Help your child bake pumpkinseeds. 1. Grease pan. 2. Place seeds on pan. 3. Sprinkle with salt. 4. Bake at 350° F (180° C) until lightly browned.
24. Have your child name safety rules for trick-or-treating.
25. Eat apples and drink apple cider. Help your child explain how apples become cider.
26. Gather small gourds. Clean out the insides and carve unusual designs. Insert tea lights to create mini lamps.
27. Read a seasonal story to your child. Ask your child to tell you the story in her own words.
28. Have your child draw a map of your neighborhood.
29. Bake slice-and-bake cookies with your child. Use candy corn to make faces.
30. Use a paper bag, glue, yarn, and crayons to help your child make a trick-or-treat bag.
31. Take a fall walk. Count groups of things, such as trees, mailboxes, or cars on the street.

Name ______________________________

OCTOBER READING LOG

Title	Author	Comments
1.		
2.		
3.		
4.		
5.		
6.		
7.		
8.		
9.		
10.		

SOMETHING TO HOWL ABOUT!

Name ______________________________

Date ______________________________

SWEET SUCCESS!

Name ______________________________

Date ______________________________

FALLING INTO GOOD HABITS!

Chart's Purpose ______________________________ **Name** __________________________

FALL IS FUN

OCTOBER BULLETIN BOARDS

Use the ghost shapes found on page 21 to create the following October bulletin boards.

Ghost Writers

Students write ghost stories on the lined ghost, then decorate the plain ghost cover with construction paper, fabric scraps, sequins, buttons, etc. Staple the two together. Instead of writing a story, younger students may finish a sentence that describes the ghosts they decorated, such as "My ghost wears a pink hat." Add detail to your bulletin board by covering the background with black paper. Place green paper across the bottom for grass. You may want to add a haunted house, a yellow moon, or clouds in the sky.

"Boo"-tiful Work

Have students write words that rhyme with the word *boo* on the ghost patterns and display on the bulletin board.

Use the ghosts to feature special student work from other areas of your curriculum, such as math work or a spelling test. Students pick their best work from the previous week to be displayed on the bulletin board.

Ghostly Math

Create a math center by having students write math story problems on the ghost patterns. Provide an answer key and a pocket in which students can place their answers.

Friendly Ghosts

Watch a cartoon starring Casper, the Friendly Ghost, or view the live-action movie version of the story. Have students brainstorm other ways in which Casper could be friendly. Write "friendly" words on blank ghost patterns and use them to make a border around a bulletin board. On the lined ghost patterns, have students write short stories about a time when they were friendly. They may also write a new story about how Casper was friendly. Display on the bulletin board with your "friendly" words.

Ghost Town

As an art project, have students create a ghost town. Each student should design one element of the town out of construction paper. When finished, assemble the whole town on a bulletin board, adding ghost cutouts as accents.

GHOSTLY SHAPES

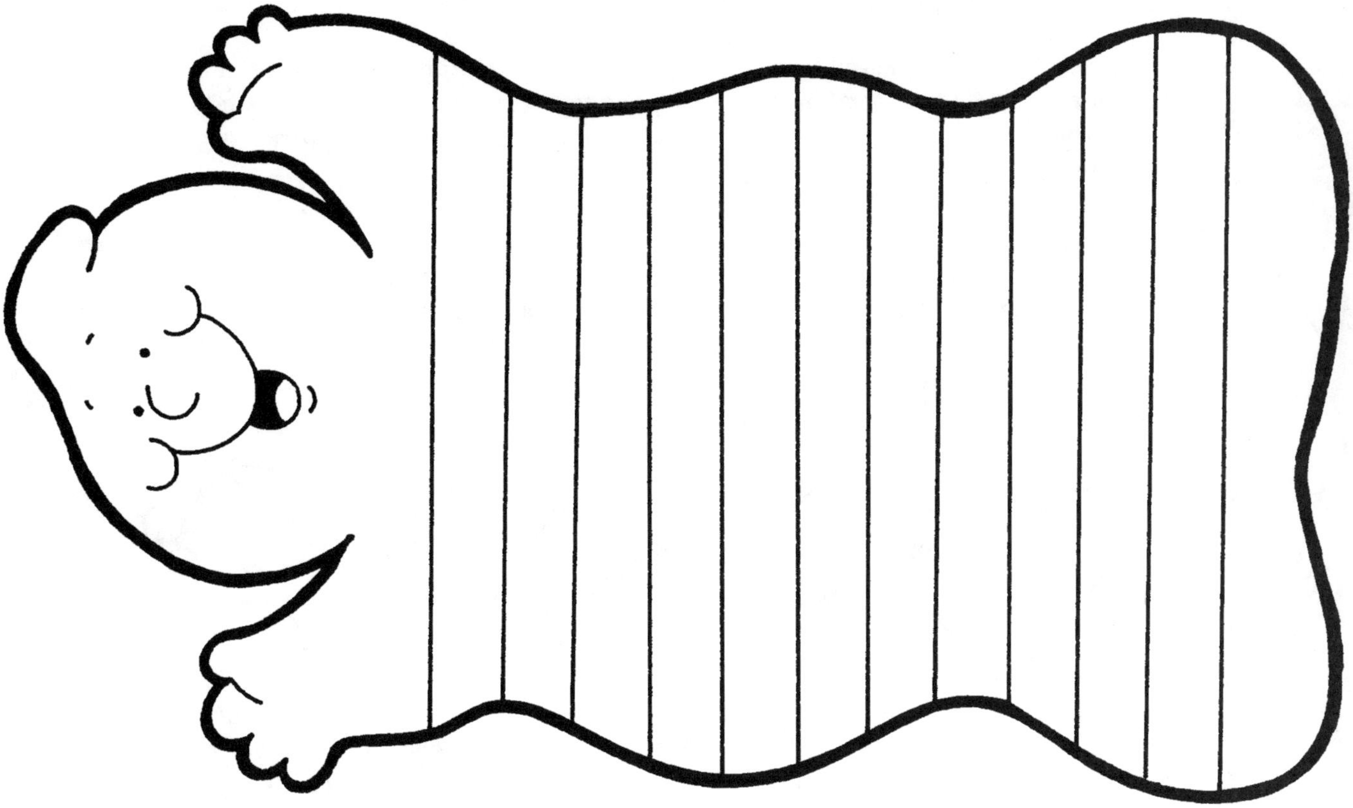

MORE BULLETIN BOARDS

Raking in the Good Work

On a leaf reproducible from page 39, have students write words that rhyme with the word *fall*. Display.

Use leaves to show homework progress for the month. Create a large tree out of tag board and place on a bulletin board or wall. Using the leaf pattern, have students add leaves with their names to a pile under the tree. Each leaf represents one homework assignment completed.

Leafing Out

Take a field trip to a local park or tree-filled area near your school. Have students collect fall leaves that are in good condition. Use a nature guide or encyclopedia to identify each leaf. You may wish to create an identification chart for students, showing outlines of common leaves. Students should create name tags for each of their leaves. Display the leaves and tags on a bulletin board.

Leafing Through Great Books

Reproduce the leaf patterns from page 39 on fall-colored construction paper. Create a bulletin board titled "Leafing Through Great Books." Also reproduce one achievement chart for each student (page 17). Attach the charts to a bulletin board. Create pockets out of folded paper and attach to the bulletin board. Label pockets fiction and nonfiction. Write titles of various books from your classroom or school library on the reproduced leaves. During free time, students may pick a leaf from a pocket and read the book. Each book read earns a fall sticker for the student's achievement chart. Students who fill their charts receive an award, seasonal candy, or a no-homework pass.

Leaf Frog Math

Create a math center by writing math sentences on paper leaves. Attach the leaves to a low-hanging bulletin board. Provide frog cutouts with the answers to the math sentences written on them. Students sort through the frogs to find the correct answer. Students then use thumbtacks or pushpins to attach the correct frog after the number sentence. To make problems more challenging, provide math story problems that students must solve using the leaf sentences and frog answers. Challenge students to write their own math stories for their classmates to solve.

PUMPKIN-PATCH FUN

Help motivate students to do their best work with this activity-board idea.

1. Cover a large bulletin board or wall with green paper.
2. Cut the words PUMPKIN-PATCH KIDS from orange paper and place at the top of the display.
3. Use the pattern below to cut one pumpkin for each student from orange construction paper.
4. Cut black eyes, a nose, and a mouth for each pumpkin. Keep at the teacher's desk.
5. Have students write their names on the pumpkins and place them on the bulletin board. As students complete specific tasks, they may add eyes, noses, or mouths until the jack-o'-lanterns are complete.

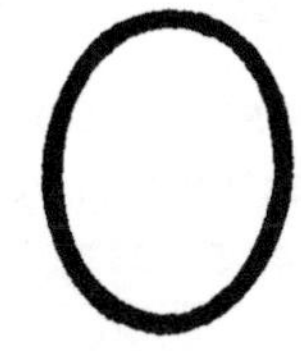

eye

nose

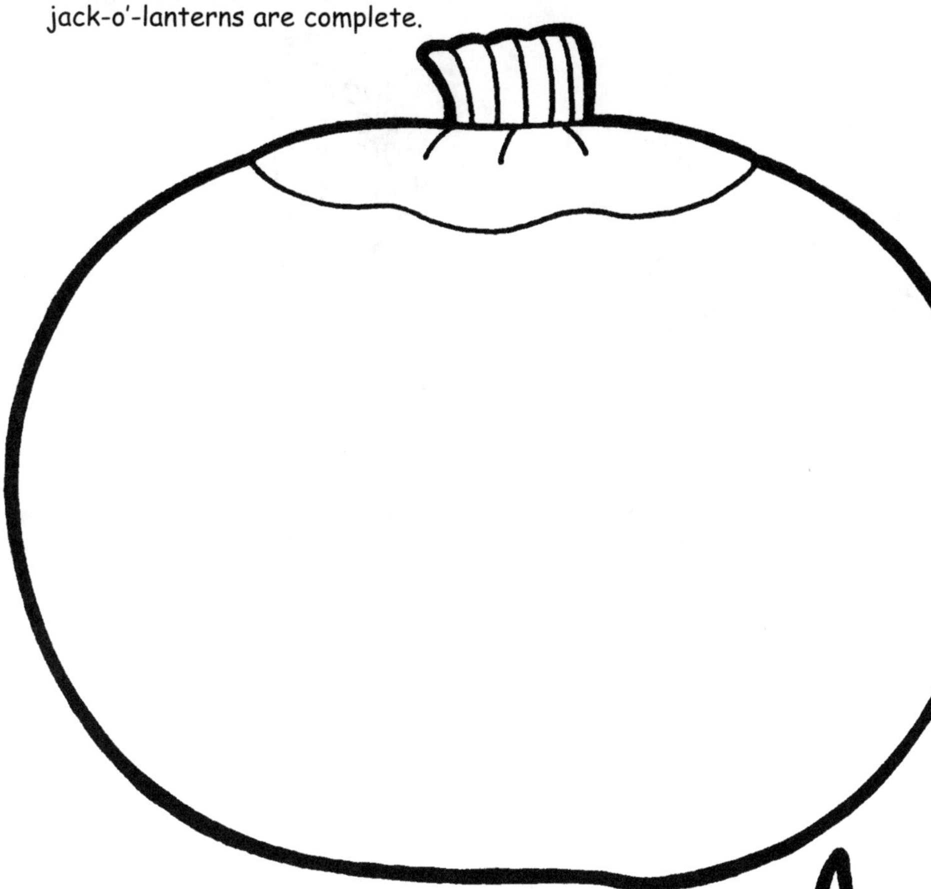

mouth

More pumpkin-pattern ideas:

1. Cut a pumpkin for each student. Have students design their own jack-o'-lantern faces to display.
2. Cut two pumpkins for the front and back of a shape book. Fill with lined paper cut in the same pumpkin shape. Place the books in a center for student poetry writing.

LITERATURE FOCUS

Read the following literature selections during the month of October.

Gackenbach, Dick. *Harry and the Terrible Whatzit.* New York: Seabury Press, 1977.

This story is about a boy who imagines a whatzit is living in his basement. A great follow-up activity is to have students draw and/or write about what they think is really in Harry's basement. Glue half a sheet of lined paper to the bottom of plain white drawing paper. Then take a tan or brown sheet of paper, cut, and glue to look like an opening door. Students then draw their version of the whatzit inside the door flap. They write about what happened to Harry on the lined paper. When finished, put the pages together to make a class book entitled, "What Did Harry's Whatzit Look Like?"

As an extension, have students use the same idea to write about something of which they are afraid. This could be a monster under the bed, lightning, dogs, or the dark. Have students use the door to draw a picture of their fear. Share these writings as a class.

Winters, Kay. *The Teeny Tiny Ghost.* New York: HarperCollins Publishers, 1997.

This story is about a tiny ghost who is afraid of Halloween and of scaring people. It is written in a pattern that is easy to imitate in a follow-up writing activity. Students write and illustrate their own versions of the pattern the story follows, such as "The teeny tiny ____________ and his teeny tiny ____________ went to a teeny tiny ____________." (Younger students may dictate their ideas to an older learning buddy or adult helper.) Put the student pages together in a class book entitled, "Our Teeny Tiny Stories." If students choose to write about a teeny tiny ghost, utilize the ghost pattern on page 21.

Bond, Felicia. *The Halloween Performance.* New York: Harper Trophy, 1987.

Schweninger, Ann. *Halloween Surprises.* New York: Puffin Books, 1986.

Read these two easy books together. Have students share their fall traditions. Then have students create a comic book-like layout (similar to *Halloween Surprises*) for their own book of Halloween or fall traditions.

LITERATURE FOCUS (CONT.)

Titherington, Jeanne. *Pumpkin Pumpkin.* New York: Mulberry Books, 1986.

This story contains a very simple explanation of the growth process of a pumpkin. Read the story to younger students. Then have each student plant a pumpkinseed in a foam cup and place in a well-lit window. Students then write their own pumpkin-planting stories.

Gibbons, Gail. *The Pumpkin Book.* New York: Holiday House, 1999.

This book shows how a pumpkin grows from a seed. Here are some possible follow-up activities.

- Make pumpkin muffins or bread.
- Carve a class pumpkin. Save the seeds and bake for a snack. Separate seeds from the pulp, place seeds on a greased pan, sprinkle with salt, then bake at 350° F (180° C) until lightly browned.

- Place an egg carton and a container of dried pumpkinseeds in a math center. Write twelve math problems on small pieces of paper. Place one in each egg section. Students place the correct number of seeds in the sections to answer the problems.
- Plant pumpkinseeds at school or have students take them home to plant.

Maestro, Betsy. *Why Do Leaves Change Color?* New York: HarperCollins, 1994.

In this book, learn about different kinds of leaves and how they change color. Go on your own leaf-collecting expedition to a nearby park. There are instructions in the back of Maestro's book for doing leaf rubbings and for pressing leaves between wax paper. Both make great art projects. See the activity on page 22, "Leafing Out," for another leaf-collecting idea.

Robbins, Ken. *Autumn Leaves.* New York: Scholastic Press, 1998.

This book contains more details about leaves and includes beautiful photographs of different leaves and trees. Have students collect leaves to label and share with the class. Leaves are also wonderful for making prints on paper or cloth. Lightly paint the veiny side of the leaf with a brush, flip over, and press onto paper. For less mess, carefully place a sheet of paper over the painted leaves and then press.

*See the Special Days section for Columbus Day books.

LITERATURE FOCUS (CONT.)

Choral Readings

A great way to get students interested in poetry and to help reading fluency is by doing choral readings. A choral reading is when a selection is read aloud by a group of students. At first, the readings should be done as a class. When the students are more familiar with the piece, the teacher may assign parts to smaller groups. Here are suggested methods for choral reading.

1. Put a copy of a poem on an overhead projector for students to read.
2. Give a "poem of the week" to the students on Monday and use it for choral readings throughout the week. On Friday, students may have a chance to read the poem alone or in a small group. They may want to be creative with their presentation by acting the poem out in some way, possibly using props.

3. Give copies of several poems to students at the beginning of the month. The leader of the day chooses the poem to read each day.
4. Incorporate poetry that fits the theme of other content areas, such as math, science, or social studies.

Here is a great resource for October poems.
Prelutsky, Jack. *It's Halloween.* New York: Greenwillow Books, 1977.

Silent Reading Club

Set aside time each day for silent reading or quietly looking at books. Make available several books that follow a basic theme or genre. Offer a small reward for reading a certain number of books in that group. Invite students to share a favorite book to stimulate other students' interest in a given title.

Post favorite books on an October bulletin board called "Great Books to Leaf Through." Have students write the titles and authors of their favorite books on leaf cutouts. Use this to keep track of how many books students read during the month of October. Students may also use the bulletin board as a resource for choosing books to read.

READING BUDDIES

Cross-age tutoring and reading are beneficial for both students involved. Establish a reading partnership with another class. Assign buddies. It is helpful for students to keep the same buddy for at least a month in order to build rapport with each other. This is a time when the older students read to the younger students, the younger students practice reading aloud to the older students, or they work together on a selected activity. You may wish to assign a fall-themed book for buddies to read. Students could complete a collaborative art activity or write an alternate ending to a story. A partnership with another class can also be used for field trips, outdoor activities, science explorations, or art projects. The following are some suggestions for October activities.

Spider Buddies

- Use page 28 to have each buddy pair make a booklet about spiders. The younger students do the coloring, and the older students put the books together and read them to their buddies.
- While students are working on the spider booklet, allow them to take turns making edible spiders at stations set up throughout the room. You may wish to post the following recipe on large chart paper. Using words and picture cues, buddies may read the recipe together.
- Have several books about spiders in your classroom library. Encourage students to read these books together.
- Have older students help younger students make spider hats (see page 38).
- Have a spider buddy race. Gather in a large open area. Have students walk like spiders in a relay race. Award the winners with plastic spider rings.

Edible Spiders

1. Mix in a small bowl:

   1 1/2 Tbs. (2.5 ml) peanut butter

   2 tsp. (10 ml) nonfat dry milk

   1 tsp. (5 ml) honey

2. Form the ingredients into a ball.
3. Roll in crushed cereal.
4. Place on 1/2 graham cracker.
5. Add eight Chinese noodles for legs and raisins for eyes.
6. Enjoy!

Name ____________

4 Insects get stuck in the webs. The spiders spin silk around the insects and eat them for dinner!

Spiders are not insects.
Insects have six legs.
Spiders have eight legs.

2

Spiders spin sticky webs
to make homes and
to catch food.

3

A HALLOWEEN PUPPET PLAY

Perform this puppet and action play as a class or in small groups. To make the puppets, duplicate page 30 for each student. Give each student five craft sticks. Have students color, cut out, and glue each puppet to a stick. Have students use the puppets while you read the play aloud. Students hold up the correct puppet(s) for each part of the play and make the sound effect in parentheses. You may also choose to have them repeat dialogue. If you choose to perform the play in small groups, each student may play a different part. As a follow-up activity, students may make up their own puppet shows using the puppets. They could perform for the rest of the class or for a reading buddy group.

Halloween Night

It was a spooky Halloween night. The wind howled through the trees. (Students say, "shhh-shhh-shhh-whoo-whoo-whoo.")

Michael and Lucy were invited to a Halloween party at their neighbors' house. Their footsteps echoed as they walked up the quiet street. (Students tap their feet on the floor.) As they came to the house, Lucy exclaimed, "Look, Michael!"

A witch jumped out of the bushes and cackled, "Heh-heh-heh-heh." (Students repeat.) Then she ran quickly into the house with her broom behind her (Students say, "swoosh-swoosh-swoosh.")

Almost immediately, Michael yelled, "Look, Lucy!" There, in an upstairs window, appeared a white ghost. In a hideous voice, it shrieked, "Boo!" (Students repeat.) Then a huge pumpkin on the porch began to barrel down the steps toward them. (Students make bumping noises.)

Michael and Lucy were so frightened that they began to run away. (Students tap feet quickly.) Just then, the porch light came on, and they heard a loud, "Happy Halloween!" When they turned around, they saw that the witch, the ghost, and the pumpkin were really their friends in costumes.

Michael and Lucy called, "We knew it was you!" But to each other they said, "Whew!" (Students make "whew" sound.)

HALLOWEEN PLAY PUPPETS

WRITING ACTIVITIES

Make a bare fall tree out of tag board or construction paper and place on a wall or bulletin board low enough for students to reach. Use the leaf and apple patterns on page 39 to provide a writing center that helps students practice writing detailed sentences. Make copies of the patterns out of fall-colored construction paper. Write a story starter on one side of each leaf or apple and a word bank on the other. Choose from the words at the bottom of this page. Attach the leaves and apples to the tree branches with pushpins. Students remove an item when they need a story starter. Encourage them to use as many words from the Word Bank as possible.

Story Starters

Picking apples is...

Some friends went trick-or-treating and...

A moonlit pumpkin patch...

At the hayride,...

A bat swooped low...

The pumpkin pie...

I was eating an apple when...

The wind got colder and clouds filled the sky as...

Every Halloween, I carve a funny pumpkin that...

As the trick-or-treaters started down the street,...

The leaves fell from the tree and...

The girls were walking through the crowded pumpkin patch when...

An owl hooted in the tree when...

My mom always makes caramel apples and...

When the smoke detector went off,...

The first things Columbus saw...

On our trip to the fire station,...

The land was very green and...

The natives greeted the sailors...

When the sailor shouted, "Land ho!",...

Word Bank

ladder	firefighter	voyage	yummy	ship
sweet	orange	hot chocolate	pumpkin	ocean
cider	pick	excited	oven	voyage
candy	vines	sailors	dark	water
costumes	horses	black	cold	fire

THE BAT MOBILE

Materials Needed:

colored poster or tag board

black marker

yarn or string

a clothes hanger

mobile patterns

Go "bat-ty" for this Halloween creative writing idea.

To make the bat mobile:

1. Enlarge the bat pattern and cut from black poster board.
2. Enlarge the moon, pumpkin, apple, leaf, and candy corn, and cut from poster or tag board.
3. Add details with a black marker.
4. Write creative writing activities on each object as follows:
   - **moon**—Write a poem about the fall moon.
   - **pumpkin**—Make as many words as you can from the letters in the word *Halloween.*
   - **apple**—Make up a recipe that uses apples.
   - **leaf**—Write a story about why leaves fall off the trees in fall.
   - **candy corn**—Write a story about a candy corn factory.
5. Punch holes, attach colored yarn, and hang the cutouts from the bat.
6. Attach colored yarn to the top of the bat and hang as a mobile.
7. Place in a writing center.

FALL POETRY

Use the following pattern to reinforce lessons on adjectives, nouns, and verbs.

1. Have students brainstorm a list of fall adjectives, nouns, and verbs. Post the lists on a chalkboard or overhead projector.
2. Give each student a copy of the poem pattern below. Students should write adjectives on the first blank of each row, nouns on the second blank, and verbs on the third blank. These words should form statements about fall.
3. Have students make a large fall shape, such as a leaf, pumpkin, ghost, or bat, with orange yarn on black construction paper. Details may be added with scrap paper, buttons, glitter, sequins, etc. Space should be left inside the shape for the poem pattern below.
4. Cut out the poem and glue inside the fall shape.
5. Display on a bulletin board.

Sample Fall Word List

apple	trees	dark	night	cold
pumpkin	spooky	air	turn	light
leaves	fall	colorful	creepy	sway
cider	drink	costume	tricky	exciting

WHEN IS FALL?

When ____________ ____________ ____________

And ____________ ____________ ____________

When ____________ ____________ ____________

And ____________ ____________ ____________

THEN IT'S FALL!

SCIENCE FOCUS–BATS

October is a great time to study bats. Here are some activities that will help your students learn about bats while having fun at the same time.

Bat Fact Puzzles

Many students have misconceptions about bats. As a class, make a list of statements students think are factual about bats. Use the bat fact puzzle on page 35 to help students sort out the bat facts from fiction. Follow up with a discussion about what new bat facts students learned. A great book to read about bats, which includes actual photographs, is *Amazing Bats* by Frank Greenaway (New York: Dorling Kindersley, 1991). This book would most likely help answer any questions students have raised.

Bats Are Different

People are often scared of bats because they don't know much about them. When people think of bats, they often think of vampire bats, or conjure up images of creatures lurking in dark corners that swoop out to frighten the unsuspecting. These frightening images, inaccurate though they are, can cause people to dislike bats. Explain the good things bats do for us (e.g., they eat mosquitoes, their waste is good for fertilizer, etc.). Then explain to your students that sometimes people also can be unfairly judged. Enlarge and reproduce the bat on page 32. Each student should write something on it that makes him or her different and why that difference is positive.

Comparing Bats with Birds

Read the book *Stellaluna* by Janell Cannon (San Diego: Harcourt Brace Jovanovich, 1993). This is a story about a young bat that becomes separated from its mother and is taken in by a family of birds. After reading the book to the class, discuss with the class the similarities and differences between bats and birds. Record class answers on a Venn diagram. Students then make their own Venn diagrams comparing bats to other animals of their choice.

BATS—FACT OR FICTION?

Cut out the puzzle pieces and put them together to form a bat. The pieces that make the right wing include facts about bats. The pieces that make the left wing are fiction.

MATH FOCUS

More Bat Fun

1. Use the bat pattern to trace and cut bats from black construction paper.
2. Fold the wings closed.
3. Write a math problem on the outside of the closed wings.
4. Write the answer on the inside of the bat.
5. Students try to solve the problem before opening the bat to check the answer.
6. Place the folded bats in a math center.

October Estimations

If you have an estimation jar or station in your room, here are some great October fillers: candy corn, black plastic spiders or bats, pumpkinseeds, black licorice, pumpkin-shaped erasers, and orange gumdrops. At the end of the first week, sort a few of the students' estimations into "too high" and "too low" categories. This will guide estimations for the following weeks. After students have made their estimations, count the items by tens and ones. Determine as a class which estimates are the closest. If the item is something the students may keep, decide as a class how to divide the contents of the jar equally.

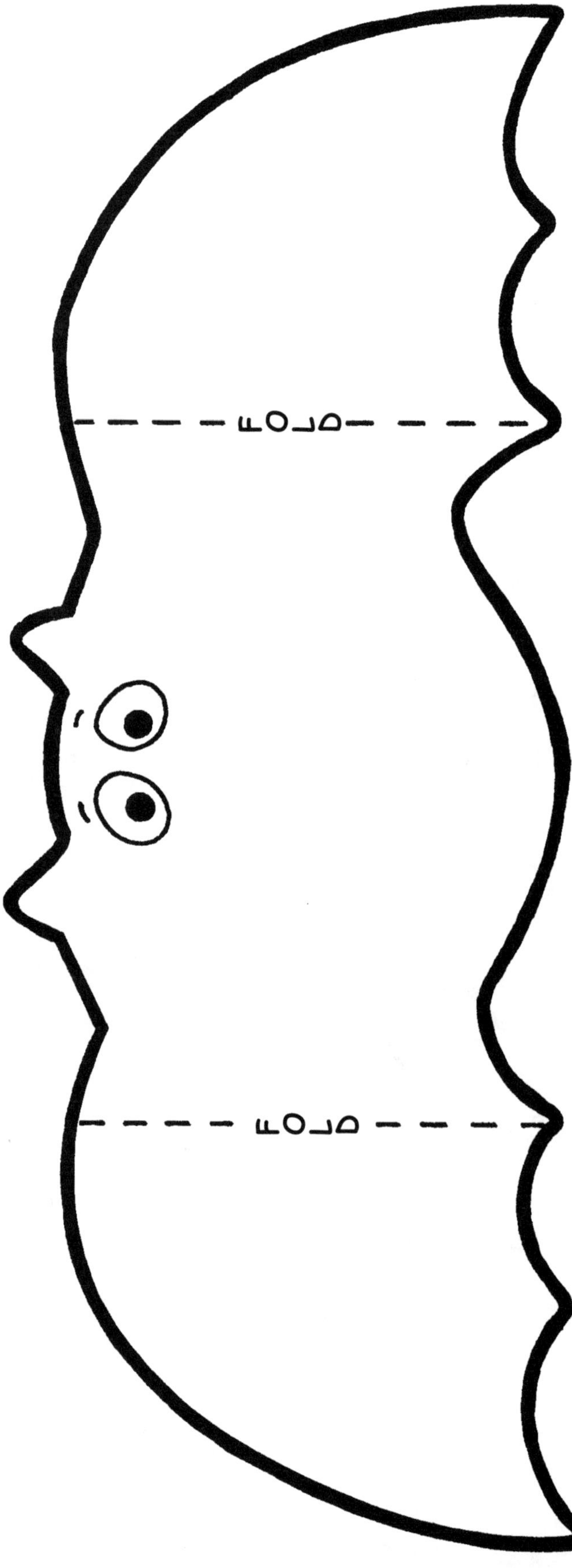

GRAPHING IDEAS

Here are some fun activities that will help your students make and interpret graphs.

How Big Is That Pumpkin?

Bring a large pumpkin to class. Have students look at the pumpkin in small groups and estimate how big around the pumpkin is by cutting a piece of string or yarn to the size they think will fit around the pumpkin. Students then compare their strings to the actual pumpkin size. Create "too big," "too small," and "just right" categories. Tape the strings on a graph according to how well students estimated. Students can also estimate the weight of the pumpkin by placing their names on a graph with their estimates. Weigh the pumpkin and compare student estimates with the actual weight.

Tricks or Treats?

Have students graph their choices for favorite Halloween candy. Put wrappers of several popular candies across the bottom of a large piece of tag board and have students write their names above their favorite choices. Identify the most and least favorite. Write math questions to ask the students based on the results of the graph, such as "How many more students liked jellybeans than bubble gum?"

What Size?

Create an estimation graph using the size of Columbus's ships: the Niña—15 m, Pinta—17 m, and Santa María—18 m. Show students a meter stick. Then have them guess the length in meters of one the ships. Graph the results. Then take students out into a large hallway or gymnasium. To demonstrate the actual length of the ship, have students lay head-to-toe on the floor. You may also wish to create a graph comparing correct and incorrect estimations of how many students were needed to represent the length.

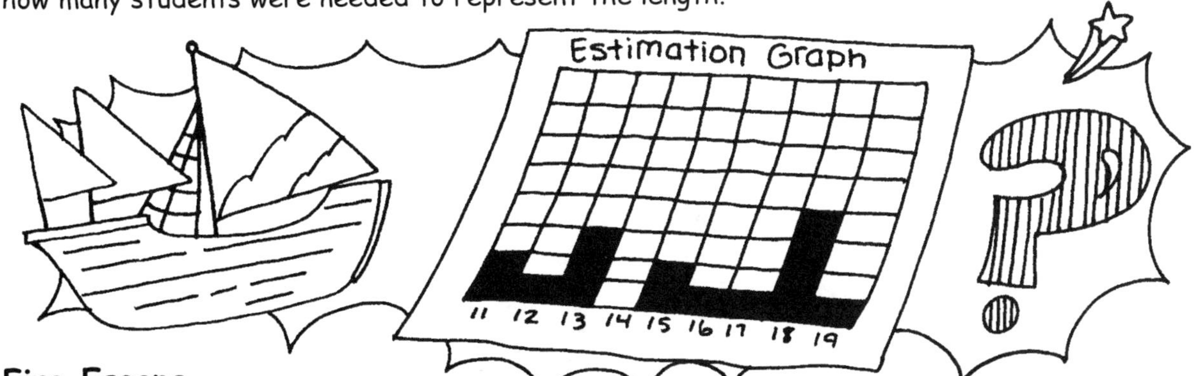

Fire Escape

Help students measure various fire escape routes from your classroom to the different school exits. Students then plot the various distances on a vertical bar graph to determine the shortest way out of school. Compare this with your mandated fire exit door. Are they the same? Why or why not?

ART ACTIVITIES

Here are some October art activities that can be done as a class or placed in an art center for students to complete individually.

Paper Bag Owl

Materials Needed:

brown paper lunch bags

orange, yellow, and brown paper

black markers

old newspaper

yarn or string

1. Cut and paste an orange beak and brown wings (triangles) and orange or yellow eyes (circles) on one side of the bag.
2. Draw "feathers" on the owl with marker.
3. Stuff with newspaper.
4. Tie yarn around the bottom to close.

Fall Family Tree

Materials Needed:

silhouette of fall tree

leaf pattern (page 39)

colored construction paper

1. Cut out a silhouette of a bare fall tree from colored paper and glue on a background, or draw a fall tree on a piece of butcher paper.
2. Cut out one leaf for each member of your immediate family. Write a name on each leaf.
3. Glue the leaves on the tree branches. (Older students may want to include extended family members.)

A Spider Hat

Materials Needed:

black construction paper

cotton balls (two per student)

1. Cut a black construction paper strip to fit each student's head.
2. Staple into a circle.
3. Give each student a piece of black paper to cut into eight strips and fold to make a bend in each.
4. Students glue the strips to the headband as legs.
5. Students cut out two eyes. Glue above the band to show a semi-circle. Give each student two cotton balls to glue in the center of each eye.

LEAFING AROUND

SPECIAL DAYS

Fire Prevention Week—first or second week

Following a class discussion about fire safety, make a bulletin board or display with a firefighter holding a running hose. Cut several water puddles out of blue paper and have students write fire-safety tips on each. Display them with the firefighter. Here are some other activities for Fire Prevention Week.

- Visit your local fire station.
- Invite someone from the fire department to your class to discuss safety rules and display equipment.
- Take a class walk through school and observe fire alarms, smoke detectors, extinguishers, and sprinkler systems.
- Discuss emergency telephone numbers.
- Practice what to do at home in case of a fire (e.g., the "stop, drop, and roll" technique, having a meeting place for all family members, etc.)
- Make home escape plans.
- Reproduce the fire hat pattern on page 42. On the hat, have students write how they can help to prevent fires or why they would want to be a firefighter. Display on a bulletin board.

Columbus Day—October 12 (observed the Monday preceding)

October 12, 1492 was the day Christopher Columbus and his crew landed in America. Here are some activities for celebrating Columbus's contributions to history.

- Read a book about Christopher Columbus and his accomplishments. *Christoper Columbus* by Stephen Krensky (New York: Random House, 1991), discusses in detail what the voyage was like for Columbus and his crew. *The Discovery of the Americas* by Betsy and Giulio Maestro (New York: Lothrup, Lee & Shepard Books, 1991) has an informative section about Columbus, as well as other important explorers. Older students will be able to compare Columbus's voyages with others described in the book.
- Make words out of the letters in the name *Christopher Columbus.*
- Make a picture depicting Columbus's three ships sailing toward shore as they arrived in America. Make copies of the ships on page 41 for the students to incorporate into their pictures. Provide blue construction paper for the background and other colored scraps for students to add detail to their pictures. Older students may write stories to go with their pictures about what they think it was like for Columbus and his crew to finally reach land.
- List key words about Columbus on the chalkboard or overhead projector and have students put them in alphabetical order. Use *discover, America, island, Pinta, Niña, Santa María, Columbus, land,* and *October.*
- Have students plan a voyage of discovery to another land. Have them list supplies they'll need to take along, how long the trip will take, and what they'll do when they get there. Students could also draw pictures or create collages to illustrate their voyages.

SAILING TO AMERICA

FIGHTING FIRE

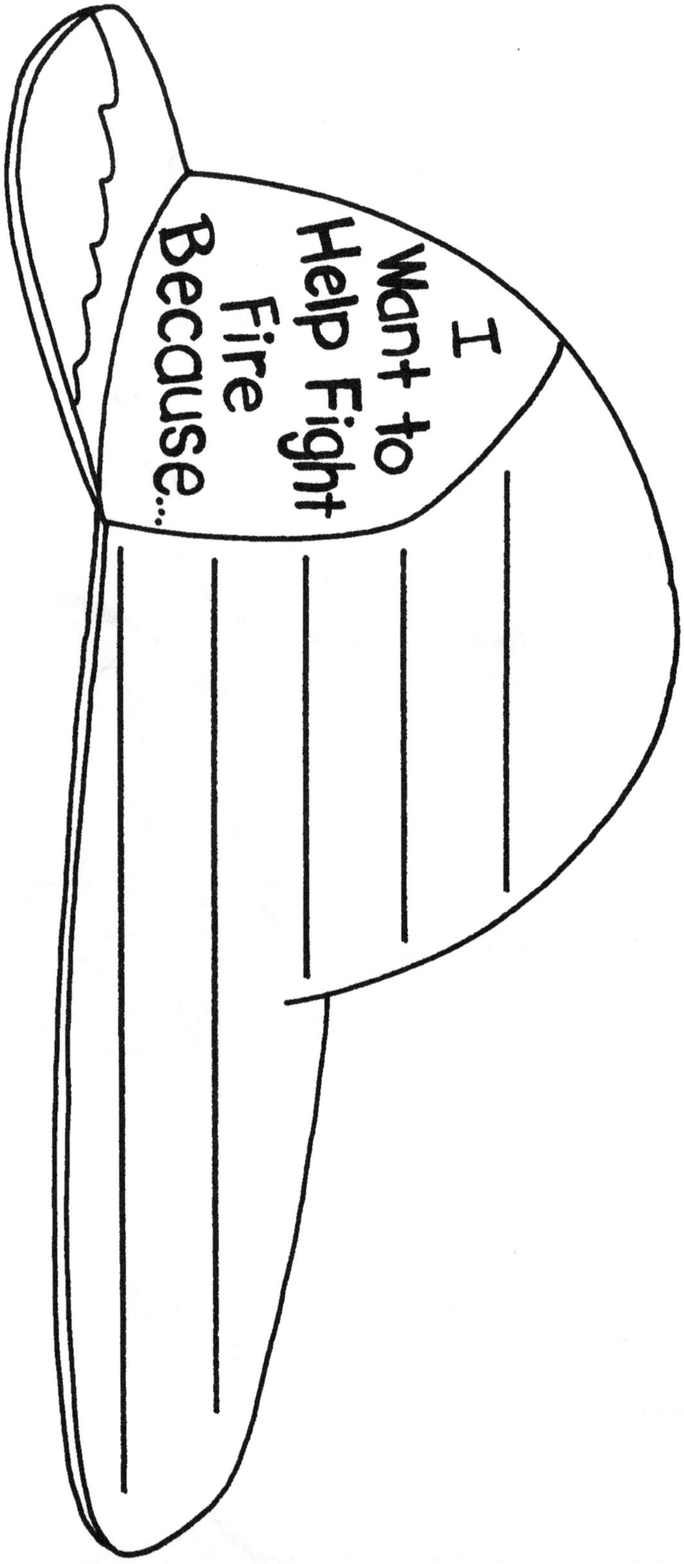

SPOOKY HOUSE

Use this as an activity page throughout the month. In the windows, write activities, such as math problems, creative writing starters, spelling words, science vocabulary, or art ideas. Cover these directions when duplicating, and use this space for writing directions for the activities.

A HALLOWEEN GAME

Materials Needed:

- colored poster board
- black marker
- orange construction paper
- white tag board
- cotton balls

To Make:

1. Copy and enlarge the game board on page 45. Color with markers and paste on a larger orange poster board. Or enlarge on an opaque projector. Color and paste to make a much larger board for more than two players.
2. Cut six pumpkins from orange construction paper or tag board. Use a black marker to make eyes and a nose.
3. On two pumpkins, draw a smile with one tooth. On two more pumpkins, draw a smile with two teeth. On the last two pumpkins, draw a smile with three teeth.
4. Shuffle and place the pumpkins facedown by the game board.
5. Out of tag board, make sets of game cards that are numbered and include questions. Game cards could include math problems, questions about a science topic, or literature connections.
6. Place a bag of cotton balls by the game board. Use a colored marker to individualize the ghost markers.

To Play:

1. Students start with their markers at the man. Players take turns picking a pumpkin card and a question card. If the question is answered correctly, the player moves the number of spaces that matches the number of teeth on the pumpkin.
2. If the question is answered incorrectly, the player does not move.
3. The first player to reach the spooky house wins the game.

THROUGH THE PUMPKIN PATCH

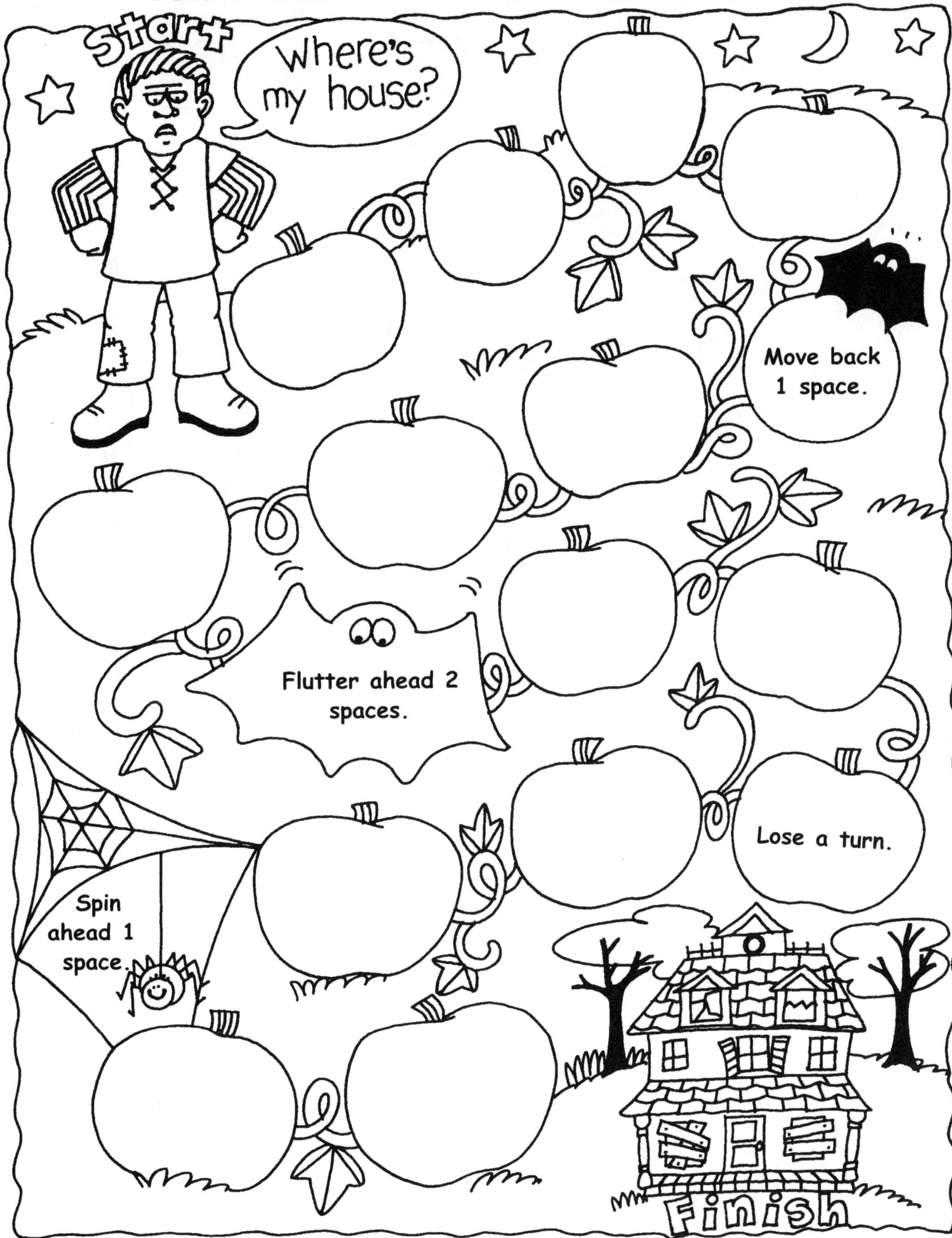

Name ____

FALL HUNT

Color the hidden pictures. Count each group and write the number in the correct box.

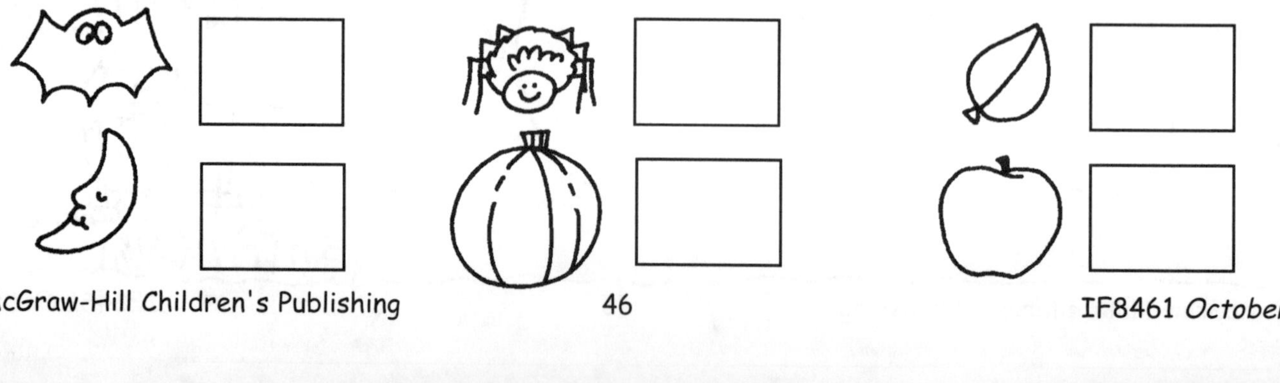

Name ____________________

HALLOWEEN PUZZLE

Read each clue. Write the correct word in the puzzle space.

Down

1. You wear me.
3. I taste good on apples.
4. I spin my own home.

Across

1. I am made of apples.
2. What you say on Halloween is "________-or-treat"
5. I grow on a tree.
6. You get me on Halloween.

Words

cider
apple
costume
spider
trick
caramel
candy

Name ______________________

SPOOKY SEARCH

Circle the 14 hidden words in the puzzle. Check off each word as you find it.

trick	lantern	costume	treat	mask
leaves	candy	boo	spider	Halloween
apples	pumpkin	bat	cat	

c	o	s	t	u	m	e	s	l	s
b	m	j	b	b	s	h	l	a	p
h	a	l	l	o	w	e	e	n	i
t	s	q	m	o	u	r	a	t	d
x	k	m	b	a	t	v	v	e	e
c	a	n	d	y	z	o	e	r	r
p	u	m	p	k	i	n	s	n	c
a	p	p	l	e	s	z	n	s	a
t	r	i	c	k	t	r	e	a	t